The Veil Of Isis

Helena Blavatsky: Mother Of The New Age

Written and illustrated
(using historical sources)

by

Jane Schauer

KREAV PUBLISHING

This edition published in 2011 by
KREAV Publishing,
Canberra, Australia.

ISBN 978-0-9804633-5-4

Madame Helena Blavatsky

Born 1831 in the Ukraine
Died 1890 in London

Helena Blavatsky was born into a well-off Russian family.
Her strange powers enabled her to telepathically move
objects and to call spirits. Before she finally settled in
London, she lived in both the USA and India. Her life was
always full of controversy, drama and strange, mystical
events.

To her followers Helena Blavatsky was a modern Buddha.
To her critics, she was nothing more than an absurd,
promiscuous charlatan, who had ridiculous ideas about the
powers of the human mind.

Was she a great mystic or a charlatan? This book
dramatically explores this question.

Helena Blavatsky

Both Stuart and Gordon had been friends since their childhood. They met at school in India, where both their fathers had then been working. Stuart's as a diplomat and Gordon's as an executive for a large bank.

Now Stuart, who was in his mid 20's, owned a New Age shop in California. He took the occult very seriously. Usually his holidays were yoga or meditation retreats. However, this year he had decided to visit his old friend Gordon, who was a lawyer in London.

Stuart flew to London and Gordon picked him up from Heathrow Airport. He wanted Stuart to meet his girlfriend Anne, who was an orchestra conductor. They drove to the concert hall where she was rehearsing some Mahler music. Stuart and Gordon sat in the front row of the empty concert hall, listening to the orchestra rehearse.

Anne joined them when the orchestra took a break. After Gordon introduced Stuart she offered them some coffee.

As they sat drinking the coffee Stuart said, "I could feel Madame Blavatsky's presence when the music was playing just now".

A surprised Anne asked him, "Who is Madame Blavatsky?"

Stuart replied, "Oh, she is dead. But she was a profoundly knowledgeable mystic, who lived in London in the eighteen hundreds. She had extraordinary powers and knowledge. She even influenced Mahler, whose music you were playing. "

Gordon laughed and said, "I've heard of Blavatsky. It was said that she was a trickster. On the other hand, her supporters claimed she made music by just snapping her fingers and that she was visited by astral travelers."

Anne, who was a cynical person, started to get irritated. She dismissively said, "Blavatsky must have been a con artist."

Stuart objected saying, "Her great knowledge was proven by her writings, which even Einstein consulted. Madame Blavatsky often had a profound influence on people.

Anne sarcastically replied, "So do the stars of soap operas."

Paris (1884)

Madame Helena Blavatsky (53 years old, grossly overweight, ill and suffering difficulties breathing) was sitting in a Parisienne reception room. With her was a group of her followers and her sister, Vera, a writer of occult fiction. The group of followers included the American, Colonel Olcott; the Irishman, Mr Judge; the Russian, Vsevolod Solovyovl; and two Indians- the good looking Mohini and the rather crazy Babula.

The Veil of Isis

Vsevolod Solovyovl

While the group was chatting a letter was delivered to Vera. Much to the excitement and wonder of the others, Helena Blavatsky clairvoyantly read the letter while it was still sealed. As she did this sweetly tinkling astral bells could be heard faintly playing. Mohini was so amazed that he threw himself at her feet and kissed the hem of her loose robe.

Solovyov, who was a well known Russian novelist, was so excited he said loudly, "You are an amazing woman. You have extraordinary powers."

He enthusiastically added, "I have heard you are writing an important new book. Can you tell us what it is about?"

Helena calmly replied, "The book is about why the universe was created and from where humans actually came."

She then sighed and continued, "Although I am unwell, I can't die yet and get the release of death. I must keep enduring the difficulties of life in order to finish the book."

After another sigh Helena added, "Indeed, I must get back to writing it now."

She then said goodbye to the group and left the room, despite Mohini begging her to stay longer.

The next day, Solovyov called on Helena at her home.

The Veil of Isis

He begged her to teach him her knowledge and powers. She refused with an abrupt "fiddle sticks" and told the disappointed Solovyov to leave because she had work to do. However, Solovyov was determined to learn her secrets and over the next few weeks he repeatedly went to her home and tried unsuccessfully to see her. Frustrated by her continued refusal to see him, Solovyov started following Helena when she went out.

Helena confronted him and said, "Knowledge of the occult can only be given slowly to those who are entitled and suitable to receive it. And knowledge comes from with-in the seeker, as a form of illumination and understanding. To be successful in the quest for this knowledge, the seeker needs patience and a sense of humour."

Solovyov was perplexed and frustrated by Helena's explanation. He continued spying on her, hoping to learn her secrets. Then he suddenly denounced her. He spread spiteful rumors that she was a fraud, who tricked people, so that they would become her followers. Solovyov said he caught her playing some silver bells, which made the same sound as the astral music she was supposed to miraculously create.

He claimed Helena confessed to him she was a fraud and had said, "One must deceive men in order to rule them."

When Helena heard Solovyov's allegations, she was very upset and complained to her sister, "As much as I will always have followers, also I will always have such enemies,

Annie Besant

such Judases. They will make me a martyr for the truth I tell. Mud has rained on me so often that now I don't even attempt to open an umbrella to shield myself from their calumny."

London (1889)

Annie Besant was a good looking, dynamic and often charming woman. Annie was a union organiser and leading atheist who was in her early forties. She had been asked by a magazine editor to review Helena Blavatsky'srecently published book about spiritualism, which was called *The Secret Doctrine*.

Helena was very ill, but she agreed to the interview. At the start of the interview Annie was suspicious and skeptical of Helena and her book. While they talked, Helena chain smoked cigarettes, which she rolled herself.

Annie critically asked, "The theory in your book is based on hierarchies. Why should readers accept your theory, when it is so elitist and you offer so little proof for it?"

Helena discussed Annie's questions with convincing argument and entertaining wit. In her discussion she denounced both religious and scientific ideas, such as Darwinism. She called them 'clap trap and flapdoodle nonsense' and 'scientific gibberish'.

Annie was impressed and fascinated by Helena's outrageous character. Annie told Helena that she was so impressed that she would become one of her followers.

The Veil of Isis

Aunt Nadya

Helena cautioned her by saying, "Many are called, but only a few are chosen. I can only show the way to those whose eyes are open to the truth and who are full of love for all of creation."

Russia (1891)

Helena Blavatsky's aunt Nadya was puzzled because a light yellow ring that Helena had given her started changing colour and going black. Nadya tried to clean it, but the ring continued to blacken and strange noises began.

The same day, at sunset, Nadya went to her drawing room. Helena's sister, Vera, was already there reading. As Nadya walked in, the organ in the room started playing by itself. Then bells started softly tinkling and a ghostly image slowly appeared of Helena wearing white.

Nadya and Vera were alarmed by these ominous events. Their fears were justified. They soon learned that the fifty-nine year old Helena had just died.

After the orchestra rehearsal finished, the friends went to Gordon's trendy, split-level home unit, which overlooked the River Thames in the Docklands. They travelled on the scenic Docklands' railway and continued to discuss Blavatsky.

Gordon said, "When Blavatsky died, both abusive and glowing tributes were published."

With some glee, Anne made up what she imagined the abusive ones said.

Defensively, Stuart countered her sarcasm by insisting, "*The New York Daily Tribune* said one day the wisdom and scope of her teaching would be recognised."

Gordon mediated the argument by saying, "It is difficult with Blavatsky to sort out the truth, particularly about her mystical powers, which she claimed to have from a very young age."

Russia (early 1840's)

As the daughter of Baron von Hahn, Helena Blavatsky was born into a family of minor Russian-German nobility. Her father was a soldier. Her mother was a well known writer, who died when Helena was eleven.

Helena was a moody and imaginative child and her relationship with her mother was tempestuous. Demons were thought to cause her disagreeable behaviour. So Helena was exorcised a number of times to rid her of them.

When she was a young girl Helena wanted to look at a family portrait which was hung high on a wall and always covered. She had been forbidden to look at the portrait, or even ask about it. However, her curiousity got the better of her, and she piled furniture up to the level of the painting, so she could climb up.

While standing on the top layer of furniture, Helena removed the painting's cover. She was so astounded by what she saw that she jerked back. Her sudden movement caused her, and the stacked furniture, to fall to the floor. The fall knocked her out.

When Helena regained consciousness she was surprised to find that all the furniture was back where it belonged and she was unhurt. Yet she could see proof of what had just happened, because her small handprint was high up on the dusty wall, next to the picture.

When they arrived at his home in the Docklands, Gordon gave the pleasantly surprised Stuart some hash as a welcoming present. He got it especially for him, because he knew Stuart liked to smoke it and couldn't bring any on his flight.

Stuart immediately rolled a large joint. He mixed the hash with some dried herbs from the kitchen, because he didn't smoke tobacco. Then, while the sun set, the three sat on the spacious balcony overlooking the river, smoking the joint. They gazed at the view of the river and the lights of the Docklands' skyscrapers.

Stuart again brought up the subject of Blavatsky, saying, "You know Blavatsky also liked to smoke hash."

Anne, surprised, asked, "How did a Victorian lady acquire such a habit?"

The Veil of Isis

Helena Blavatsky

Stuart explained, "As a young woman, Madame Blavatsky travelled widely in the middle East. She probably picked up the habit then." He continued, "She said she travelled to study spiritualism and to develop her psychic powers."

Gordon added, "From what I know about her, she was a complex character, who could also be an absolute bitch."

Anne said interestedly, "Tell me about her bitchiness."

Georgia (1848)

At 16, Helena von Hahn was beautiful and full of life. However, she was also very vain. She ridiculed the ugliness of a man in his forties. The man was Nikifor Vassilievich Blavatsky and he was the Vice-Governor of a region in the Caucasus.

Helena's disapproving governess chastised her nastiness, saying, "Helena, you are so self-centred and you have such a temper that you will find it difficult to get a husband. Not even the man you are ridiculing would marry you."

Helena was extremely annoyed by what her governess had said and she became determined to prove her wrong.

Several days later she gloated as she conceitedly told her dismayed governess, "I got Blavatsky to propose to me and I have accepted."

The Veil of Isis

Then, later, Helena indifferently told her Aunt Nadya, "I have changed my mind. I don't want to marry Blavatsky."

Nadya was annoyed by Helena's behaviour.

She lectured her, "You must not play with Nikifor Vassilievich's feelings. You made a commitment and you must now go ahead with the marriage."

Helena went ahead with the marriage. However, during the ceremony, when the priest told Helena she must obey her husband, she muttered, "I will not."

After the wedding Helena refused to consummate the marriage. A few months later, she fled to her grandmother's house.

Helena told her grandmother, "I will kill myself rather than return to my husband."

The friends' conversation carried on over a bottle of white. Gordon poured them a glass of wine each, while Stuart rummaged in his bag for presents he had brought them. Anne was pleased with her gift, which was a large scented candle. Gordon was intrigued when he opened his present to find it was a book, *The Voice Of The Silence*, written by Blavatsky.

Stuart commented that, "It must be an omen that I chose for you a book written by Blavatsky. I am sure I can again feel her presence."

Anne made a scoffing laugh.

As Gordon perused the book, Stuart explained, "You know Blavatsky wrote the book after she had been in Tibet for a few years. It was extraordinary that she managed to get into Tibet, because then it was a closed society. She wrote the book about what she had learnt there."

Anne frowned and said, "Is there any actual proof that Blavatsky did go to Tibet?"

Stuart reverently took the book from Gordon and showed them the book's endorsement, which was written by the current Dalai Lama. He insisted, "The Dalai Lama would never have written this endorsement if there was not evidence of her visit there to study with high spiritual masters.

London (1851)

Three years after fleeing from her husband, Madame Blavatsky was working as a companion to a Countess. They were staying at what is now called the Claridge Hotel. Helena, who was a gifted pianist, was depressed and was playing some sombre music.

The Countess did not like the music. She said, "That music is so sad. Is something the matter?"

Helena sighed and said, "Since I left my husband, I have travelled to many strange places. Always I have been seeking the philosopher's stone of truth about the meaning of life. I have studied many things, including astrology and crystals. Yet I have not found the truth I have sought. All that has happened is that I have had the social hollowness knocked out of me."

The countess wanted an amusing companion. She was irritated by Helena's depression and she was not interested in philosophy.

She commanded Helena, "Go for a walk. Exercise will cheer you up. A miserable companion is a poor companion."

Helena walked for a while and then stood on Waterloo Bridge. She stared at the murky Thames River and contemplated suicide. Then suddenly she saw a vision of a tall, handsome, Indian man.

The ghostly image talked to her saying, "I will be your guide and help you find the truth you seek."

The vision then faded and Helena felt a peaceful calm.

A few days later, she was walking in a London street when she saw the same tall, mystic guide in the flesh. He was walking toward her with a group of richly dressed Indian princes. She hurried towards him, wanting to talk to him again. As he saw her coming, he signalled Helena not to talk to him. She stood and looked at him respectfully as he walked past her.

The Veil of Isis

Master Morya

Later, when she was walking in Hyde Park, she again encountered her guide, Master Morya. This time he was alone and he talked to her.

He told Helena, "I am one of the Great White Brotherhood. I will guide you in the important work you have to do to assist in the development of world peace."

Helena listened to him with deference while he explained, "You must prepare for this work by studying for 3 years in Tibet."

"The friends continued to argue about whether Blavatsky was a mystic, or a trickster, and if she had learnt new psychic powers in Tibet.

Anne sarcastically asked, "To what purpose did Blavatsky put her new, supposedly divine, powers?"

Gordon mischievously replied, "Well, initially she entertained her family and friends."

Russia (1860)

At 29 Helena Blavatsky was a beautiful woman. She told a gathering of her family that she was practicing with her psychic powers and that she was learning to control her powers.

Her disbelieving brother, Leonid, asked, "What can you do?"

The Veil of Isis

The Veil of Isis

Helena replied, "I can change the weight of objects. I can make them heavier, or lighter."

Leonid laughed and said, "Well show us what you can do."

When she agreed to show him, the others were very interested.

Helena stared at a small table for a few minutes and then instructed her brother, "Try to lift that table."

She continued to stare at the table as he unsuccessfully tried to lift it. Leonid got very annoyed when he could not budge the table. His friend also tried and failed. Then Leonid tried again to lift it.

As he became increasingly frustrated and struggled and strained, Helena said, "Now you will see my power."

As soon as she finished speaking, Leonid was able to suddenly lift the table. He almost fell over, because he had been tugging at the table, expecting it to be difficult to lift. He was astounded.

Helena just shrugged and said to her impressed family, "I just changed the magnetic force under the table."

A few weeks later, Vera and other members of Helena's family were entertaining guests who had heard about Helena's strange powers. One of the guests, a rather arrogant woman, whispered to her friend, "I think Madame Blavatsky fakes all the strange noises which occur when she is around. It is probably quite easy to fake them."

The Veil of Isis

Helena came into the room and immediately strange murmurings could be heard. She sat in a chair and started doing some embroidery. The woman then loudly asked her, "Can you control the noises?"

Without looking up, Helena replied, "Yes". The sound changed to a banging noise.

The woman then dismissively said, "That is rather a nasty noise. Can't you make any nicer sounds?"

Helena looked up and smiled. Lovely tinkling bells were then heard.

The woman continued, "What is the best conducting material for the noises?"

Helena stared at the woman and said, "Gold."

The woman's face contorted and loud tapping noises could be heard coming from the gold fillings in her teeth. She covered her mouth with her hands and rushed out of the room in alarm and embarrassment.

Although the family were amused by the event, Vera scolded her sister, "Helena, that was not very kind."

Helena indifferently replied, "The woman was a vain toad, so I taught her a lesson."

As the friends talked about Blavatsky, Stuart rolled another joint. Anne and Gordon didn't want any more, so Stuart smoked by himself. As he smoked he said, "You know Blavatsky was the mother of the New Age."

Anne was quite amused by his statement and said, "That would make sense."

As he got up to go to the nearby bathroom, Stuart explained, "Not the young Blavatsky, but the older wiser woman."

 While Stuart was urinating, Gordon called out to him. He questioned, "What do you mean by wiser? When she was older Blavatsky lived an unhealthy life style. She took little exercise, had a poor diet, worked long hours and continually smoked. There is not much wisdom in that behaviour."

Stuart shouted back to him, "It was her ideas, not her life-style, which were wise and so important. You know many people were influenced by her ideas. Not just during her life, but after her death as well."

Then, as Stuart was shaking his penis dry, he looked over at the large bathroom mirror and in it he saw a faint image of Madame Blavatsky.

Stuart was initially slightly spooked by the image, but then he became highly excited. He rushed out of the bathroom to where Gordon and Anne and were sitting. He repeatedly, and excitedly, kept saying, "I have just seen Madame Blavatsky. She is in the bathroom."

The Veil of Isis

William & Horatio Eddy

At first Gordon was puzzled by Stuart's bizarre behaviour, but then he became amused, because in Stuart's excitement and rush to leave the bathroom, he had left himself slightly exposed. While pulling a funny face, Gordon pointed to Stuart's zipper region and his slightly exposed penis.

Anne poked fun at Stuart saying, "You are crazy! It is just a fantasy! You are off your face with hash and hallucinating. What was Blavatsky doing in the bathroom? Was she checking you out?"

She then convulsed in laughter.

United States (1873)

When she was 43, Helena arrived in the United States. She was a very self confident person who dressed flamboyantly. She was also overweight and a chain smoker.

In New York, Helena read an article about two mediums, the Eddy brothers, William and Horatio. They were uneducated farmers in Vermont. She went to visit them in their gloomy, old farmhouse.

At the farm she met Colonel Henry Olcott. He was a 42 year old lawyer, who had recently been one of the official investigators of President Lincoln's assassination. He was now interested in spiritualism, which was why he was visiting the Eddy brothers.

The Veil of Isis

Helena Blavatsky

The Eddy brothers held a séance for their visitors. It was a serious affair, during which Helena summoned a number of different spirits. She showed she was a more skilful psychic than either William, or Horatio.

Henry Olcott was most impressed by her masterly skills. However, after the séance, he was baffled when she told him, "One should not play at the vulgar, dangerous amusement of contacting spirits of the dead."

She then said, "The only worthwhile activity is to contact the brotherhood of spiritual masters, the Adepts."

While rolling a cigarette, she explained to the awed and gullible Henry, "The brotherhood of masters are beings, such as Jesus and Buddha, whose training and absolute purity gives them super-natural powers. These Adepts are immortal, immaterial and can move about the universe. They endeavour to save humans from the evil influence of the Dark Powers. They transmit their wisdom through specially chosen human agents, such as myself. But their agents are often not believed. Instead we agents are persecuted because of the influence of the Dark Powers."

When Helena returned to New York, Henry continued to meet with her. He was one of a group of people who treated her as their guru. She was nicknamed Isis. On one occasion she was playing her piano to Henry and some others, when William Judge arrived to meet her. He was a handsome 24 year old Irish-American lawyer.

William Judge

The Veil of Isis

The room in which Helena entertained her guests was bizarre and exotic. There were a lot of oriental objects, piles of books and papers, stuffed animals, birds and reptiles. Because Helena did not agree with Darwin's theories, the room also contained a large stuffed baboon holding a copy of Darwin's book: *The Origin Of The Species*. The baboon wore glasses and was dressed as Darwin.

On the day William Judge called, Helena amused and impressed her guests by mystically moving objects through walls and instantly copying objects. While doing this, her canaries flew freely around the room and she made witty jokes. Then, with more seriousness, she summoned a shimmering spirit who talked about the need for humans to have a universal brotherhood which did not discriminate between race, creed, sex, caste or colour.

When the spirit left, the group became animated with excitement. Some claimed what they had just witnessed was a miracle. Helena calmed the group saying, "There is no such thing as a miracle. There are only immutable laws of nature. We just do not yet fully understand all of the laws."

Helena then persuasively discussed with them what the spirit had said. She told them, "The way to achieve a universal brotherhood is to study different religions and philosophies and to find the common thread."

When Helena left the room, Henry Olcott told William Judge, "I am one of Madame Blavatsky's disciples because

The Veil of Isis

Henry Olcott

she has extraordinary gifts and she has an important mission."

William was so wonder-struck by what he had just seen and heard that he replied, "I think the world needs her important work. I will also be her disciple and assist."

Then, for months, Helena neglected her health by working long hours writing a huge book. She was quite ill at times. She said the book was about the wisdom the brotherhood of masters, the Adepts, had shared with her.

While working on her book she constantly smoked, rarely went out and mainly lived on oatmeal. She told Henry, "I have been told to write about both religion and science, because in the current slop basin of knowledge, both are misguided, the truth is a uniting of the two."

During this time, Henry once found her in a trance at her desk. Her crinkly brown hair was black and straight. Tinkling music was playing and shimmering images hovered around. As the shimmering images dissolved and the music stopped, Helena came out of her trance.

She told Henry, "I was visiting the astral library to find some important information for my book."

She later added, "Sometimes I don't need to visit the astral library because the written pages just appear on my desk. They have been sent by the masters."

Helena named her book *Isis Unveiled*. She said the book's

The Veil of Isis

Helena Blavatsky

name referred to a quotation on an ancient sculpture of the Egyptian goddess Isis. The quotation said:

"I am all that has ever been,

all that is,

all that ever shall be,

and no mortal has ever lifted my veil."

When she at last finished writing her book she said to Henry, "Writing the book was a thankless task, because it will be widely attacked by both Christians and those pretentious snobs, the scientists."

As she anticipated, the book was controversial. Her first print run sold out, but a criticism was published that it contained over 2,000 unacknowledged quotations. She dismissed the criticism by saying, "Ye gods and little fishes, I can't be held responsible for the content. I received the words spiritually."

Helena became well known and a young Georgian man, Michael Betanelly, started calling on her. He was an import and export dealer who admired her work so much that he developed an obsession for her. Even though she was much older, he asked her to marry him. She initially refused, which just made him a more ardent suitor.

Michael made numerous more proposals, telling Helena, "I just want to unselfishly adore your intellectual grandeur. I do not want any other marriage privileges."

ऒ

Then, despite not having divorced her first husband, or having any knowledge of his death, Helena married Michael. She did not find out he was destitute until after their marriage. They quickly separated.

She told her friends, "He is a selfish cad and an ass."

Michael claimed she was a fraud, saying, "I found out a lot of her book was copied from other books in her study."

The friends' rather boozy and drugged conversation proceded with a lot of interruption and over-talking. Stuart, who was very high, raved about how Blavatsky became an American citizen, because she loved liberty.

He said, "She believed the US was the key to the future."

Anne was annoyed by this overt patriotism and made a long fart sound.

Gordon countered, "Well once she was made a citizen, she deserted America almost as quickly as she deserted her husbands."

Shaking his head in disagreement, Stuart explained, "No. She wrote a huge book in America, *Isis Unveiled*. Then she left to go to India, because she believed she had important work to do there."

India (1878)

When Helena Blavatsky was 46 years old, she left the USA and went to live in India in the city of Bombay

The Veil of Isis

Henry Olcott & Helena Blavatsky

(now modern day Mumbia). Her old friend, Henry Olcott, accompanied her. He was now a slow moving and thoughtful old man.

In India, Helena smoked hashish and was outspoken in her opinions and confident about defending them. The British secret service decided she was probably a Russian spy. She was put under surveillance by the Chief of Police, Major Henderson. All her incoming letters and telegrams were read by the secret service and her outgoing letters were often confiscated.

Major Henderson was absurdly incompetent at his surveillance and it quickly became obvious to Helena that she was being watched. She decided the best way to deal with the situation was to ingratiate herself to the Major and make him her friend. She succeeded in doing this.

Helena employed a 15 year old Indian boy, Babula, to be her servant. She also employed a couple, the Coulombs, who had been her friends in Egypt. They were now destitute in Bombay and she wanted to assist them. She employed Emma Coulomb as her housekeeper and Alex Coulomb as her handyman.

Rather than being grateful, Emma and Alex were bitter about their current situation. They considered their employment to be degrading. They were resentful that when they had met Helena years ago in Egypt, she had been in trouble and they thought they had saved her.

Helena had been running a seance business, which collapsed when she was accused of fraud. She became

The Veil of Isis

desperate for money and they had helped her out with a loan. Because of this past history, the Coulombs thought that Helena owed them better treatment than employing them as very poorly paid servants.

Alex Coulomb complained to his wife Emma, "On the miserly wages she pays us, we will never be able to save enough to leave India."

Emma reassured him, "She owes us more than she pays us. Don't worry. I will take extra money for us from the housekeeping."

Helena became well known in India. She was invited to salons, where she sometimes performed mystical acts. She was referred to as the Countess, but privately Henry called her Old Horse.

Helena told him, "The British ruling class here are arrogant and stupid. They need to be shaken up. I might become a British citizen and call myself Mrs Tufmutton."

As she aged, Helena became increasingly bad tempered and egotistical, which created problems in her relationship with Henry.

Behind his back, she said to her housekeeper, Emma Coulomb, "Henry is a conceited, boring windbag."

Emma seized the opportunity to cause mischief. She ensured that Henry heard her tell her husband the unkind words that Helena had said.

The Veil of Isis

Henry was offended and angrily confronted Helena telling her "You are too often unnecessarily critical of people. You frequently cause harmful arguments. Your behaviour is detrimental to our important mission."

In response to his rebuke, Helena just winked and laughed.

Helena was interested in Buddhism and Hinduism. She visited many sacred sites and spoke to well known teachers. She enthusiastically promoted the religions. This outraged the local Christian missionaries, who subsequently wanted to discredit her.

Helena became gravely ill with both dengue fever and Bright's disease. Her illness caused her to become very bloated. She understood that she has not many more years to live and she became introspective.

She said to a dismayed Henry, "I might kick the bucket anytime."

However, her health improved for a while and she moved to a beautiful residence in Madras. She was accompanied by Henry and the resentful Coulombs. Her relationship with Henry was still rather strained.

In Madras, she worked relentlessly on a new book, *The Secret Doctrine*, which she wanted to finish before she died. She said her book was about the secret laws of the universe. Then, 6 years after Helena had first arrived in India, her illness returned so acutely that she could no longer walk.

Helena complained to her doctor, "I am like a squeezed

The Veil of Isis

Mohini M. Chatterji

out lemon."

He told her, "You must leave India and return to the cooler climate of Europe. If you don't, you will die within a few months."

Helena replied, "Then I must carry my ruin back to England."

She left India accompanied by Henry, Babula, her servant, and Mohini, a young Indian lawyer who was her disciple. The Coulombs did not accompany them. Helena had to be hoisted aboard the boat in a chair attached to a rope, because she was so grotesquely bloated and ill.

After Helena left India, the remaining board members of Blavatsky's spiritual society charged the Coulombs with fraudulently using the society's funds. In response, Emma Coulomb angrily denounced Helena. The outraged board then sacked the Coulombs. After being told of their dismissal, Alex Coulomb angrily punched one of the board members.

Because of their dismissal, the Coulombs were destitute and revengeful. Reverend Patterson, a Christian missionary, provided the Coulombs with some help. He despised Helena and had been very pleased when the Coulombs told him that she was a fraud, who could not perform miracles. Emma and Alex also confided to Reverend Patterson, and his priggish colleagues, that Helena was an immoral woman, who had many lovers. The Coulombs said that Helena had an illegitimate child. The father was probably an Italian opera singer, but it was difficult to tell because she had more than one lover at the time. The child was deformed and died young.

Emma and Alex contritely confessed to Reverend Patterson that they had been coerced into helping Helena fake her miracles – the objects and letters that mysteriously appeared and the visions of masters. The Coulombs explained that the objects and letters were put through trap doors in the walls and ceilings, which Alex had previously made. They described how the visions were created in dimly lit rooms using a doll which was moved by a long bamboo pole.

With the help of the missionaries, the Coulombs made their allegations public. Their claims caused a scandal. The board members of Blavatsky's society were horrified to find a system of holes between Helena's bedroom and the adjoining meeting room. However, the board then counter claimed that the system of holes had been made by Alex after Helena had left India. They argued that he had made the system as part of a plot to get money by discrediting Helena. As proof, the resolute board insisted that the system was unfinished and unusable. They said it was unfinished because the Coulombs' unexpected sacking had interrupted Alex's work in creating it.

The board's accusations led to a request for the system to be viewed by independent witnesses. The board declined this request. The reason they gave for their refusal was that they had already had the holes repaired.

Newspaper articles were published, which claimed that Madame Blavatsky was a fraud, whose deceits had been uncovered. An official report was released, which found Helena was an unscrupulous cheat and probably a Russian spy. When Helena was told about what had happened in India and the scandal, she was confused, nervous and upset.

She complained as she smoked a cigarette, "I have been unjustly accused of being a Russian spy because the British officials hate me. They want to discredit me because I support Indian home rule. Their report was unfairly based on what the Coulombs said and they are lying vipers."

When she was told the report described her as one of the most accomplished, ingenious and interesting imposters in history, she sadly said, "If I have ever done anything crass, it was due to my own base nature. However, the miracles I have performed were due to the guidance of the masters."

After saying this, she sat quietly for a while and lit another cigarette. As she smoked it, she regained her confidence. She then said emphatically, "I have never used fraud to promote my own or the society's financial prosperity. I am a poor woman who has no personal assets. My only income was from my writing and I have donated most of that to the society. The parasitic press just published the untruthful scandal because it sold papers."

The Veil of Isis

Helena Blavatsky

A mini-cab driver rang Gordon's doorbell and talked on the intercom. He had come to pick up Stuart, whose wealthy mother was currently in London and was expecting him for dinner. As the friends said their goodbyes, they were all in a good mood.

Gordon said, "It is hard to know what to believe about Blavatsky. Was she a trickster, a genius, a person with a phenomenal memory, or a great mystic?"

Stuart laughed and replied, "Madame Blavatsky's great genius was in collecting together and interpreting wisdom from so many different cultures and times. The real mystery is how she knew all those things." He then hugged Anne and Gordon and left.

Once Stuart had gone, Anne said, "The real mystery is why people get taken in by such bull-shitters as Blavatsky, or the modern so called channellers, who claim they are from Atlantis, or some other such ludicrous place."

Stuart got into the waiting cab. As it drove off, he saw the cab driver's face for the first time. It was reflected in the rear vision mirror. He was confounded to recognise the face. Although the driver was dressed in modern clothes, his face was that of Madame Blavatsky's guide, Master Morya. Stuart recognised him from a picture he had previously seen.

The Veil of Isis

Contemporary Opinions

William Coleman's 1883 publication, *The Sources Of Blavatsky's Writing*, stated, " . . . many readers of *Isis*, and subsequently those of her *Secret Doctrine* . . . have been misled into thinking Madame Blavatsky . . . was possessed of vast erudition; while the fact is her . . . ignorance was profound . . . The doctrines, teachings, dogmas, etc., of theosophy, as published by Helena Petrovna Blavatsky, and affirmed to be derived from the quasi-infallible Mahatmas of Thibet, were borrowed from the philosophies and religions of the past and present, with some admixture of modern science. There is nothing original . . . save the work of compilation into a composite whole . . . and the garblings, perversions, and fabrications indulged in by her in the preparation of the system of thought called theosophy."

William Judge's 1893 article, *Authorship Of Secret Doctrine*, claimed, "A good deal has been said about the writing of *Isis Unveiled*, and later of the *Secret Doctrine*, both by H. P. Blavatsky. A writer . . . took great pains to show how many books the first work seems to quote from, and the conclusion to be arrived at after reading his diatribes is that H.P.B. had an enormous library at her disposal, and of course in her house, for she never went out, or that she had agents at great expense copying books, or, lastly, that by some process or power not known to the world was able to read books at a distance . . . The last is the fact. She lived in a small flat when writing the first book and had very few works on hand . . . Those who were with her saw day after day that she could gaze with ease into the astral light and glean whatever she wanted . . . *The Secret*

Doctrine, . . . makes no disguise of the real help, . . . that the Masters had a hand in that great production."

Richard Hodson's 1885 *Report for the Society For Psychical Research* concluded that Madame Blavatsky and her associates who were "the primary witnesses to the existance of a Brotherhood with occult powers . . . have in other matters deliberately made statements which they must have known to be false, and that, therefore, their assertions cannot establish the existence of the Brotherhood in question."

On the other hand, *The Indian Chronicle* said, "We are not Theosophists ourselves . . . but we have a great respect for the founders of the Theosophical Society . . . The Christian scoffers . . . are perhaps not aware that the existence of Mahatmas . . . is universally believed throughout India."

Residence Of Blavatsky & Olcott, Bombay, India